THE COMPLETE AIR FRYER COOKBOOK WITH PICTURES

Simple and Affordable Recipes for Beginners with Tips & Tricks to Fry, Grill, Roast, and Bake Your Favorite Meals

KATHERINE LAWRENCE

Table Of Contents

Introduction

What is an air fryer?

The air fryer is simply a more powerful countertop convection oven. (However, there is a distinction to be made between air-frying and baking.) The little gadget, patented by Philips Electronics Company, claims to duplicate the effects of deep-frying using nothing more than hot air and little or no oil. According to market research company NPD Group, approximately 40% of U.S. homes will have one by July 2020. You can air-fry anything, from frozen chicken wings and handmade french fries to roasted veggies and fresh-baked cookies.

In every kitchen, counter space is in short supply. Even if you have a lot of room, it is easy to overcrowd it with the latest kitchen gadgets. You will want to create room for an air fryer, on the other hand. In that it bakes and roasts, an air fryer is comparable to an oven. Still, the difference is that its heating components are only on top and are accompanied by a huge, powerful fan, resulting in food that is very crispy in no time — and, more importantly, with less oil than deep-fried equivalents. Air fryers frequently heat up fast and cook food quickly and evenly due to a combination of a concentrated heat source and the size and location of the fan.

Another advantage of air frying is the ease of cleaning. Most air fryer baskets and racks may be washed in the dishwasher. However, we recommend an excellent dish brush, such as this one from Casabella, for those that are not dishwasher safe. It will properly get into all the nooks and crannies — which enhance air circulation! — without making you crazy.

An air fryer is a small convection oven that can be placed on your kitchen counter. It will cook everything you would cook in an oven, but the major appeal is that with very little oil (just a teaspoon), an air fryer will offer you crispy fries, wings, and veggies you never thought you would get at home, let alone without a deep fryer.

What exactly is the distinction between an air fryer and a deep fryer?

Air fryers use a high-powered fan for baking food at a high temperature, whereas deep fryers cook food in a vat of oil that has been heated to a precise temperature. Both cook food rapidly; however, an air fryer requires almost no preheat time, whereas a deep fryer might take up to ten minutes. Air fryers utilize little to no oil, but deep fryers use a lot of oil, absorbing the food. Food comes out crispy and juicy in both appliances, but they do not taste the same, mainly because deep-fried dishes are covered in batter, which cooks differently in an air fryer vs. a deep fryer. The batter needs to be sprayed with oil before cooking to help it color and crisp up in an air fryer, whereas hot oil soaks into the batter in a deep fryer. Flour-based and moist batters do not work well in an air fryer, but they work great in a deep fryer.

Is air-fried food healthy?

The flavor and texture of air-fried meals are comparable to that of deep-fried cuisine: It is crispy on the surface yet moist on the inside. However, depending on what you are cooking, you may use a small amount of oil, if any at all.

Yes, according to Good Housekeeping's Nutrition Director Jaclyn London, MS, RD, CDN, air frying is "definitely a better alternative if you commit to using only 1-2 tablespoons of a plant-based oil with seasoning and keep to air-frying veggies more than anything else." "Any appliance that assists you and your family in increasing their veggie game as we age is crucial for weight control, a decreased chance of chronic illness, and better long-term health."

Most versions do not require oil to work; however, spraying your food with cooking spray or coating it with a teaspoon or two of oil before placing it in the basket improves the texture and flavor of air-fried dishes. While it is possible to enjoy air-fried food without using any oil, the beauty of this equipment is that it only requires a minimal quantity.

A teaspoon of oil has just 40 calories (120 calories per tablespoon). The small amount of oil you use browns and caramelizes everything, resulting in extremely crispy and delicious results. And, when compared to deep-fried items, the quantity of oil used in the air fryer is almost nothing, resulting in fewer calories and saturated fat than traditional fried foods.

In an air fryer, you may cook a variety of foods.

Air fryers are quick to operate, and once you learn how they work, you can use them to heat frozen items or cook a variety of fresh dishes such as chicken, steak, pork chops, fish, and vegetables. Most meats do not require additional oil since they are inherently juicy, season with salt and your favorite herbs and spices. Use dried spices whenever possible; less moisture means sharper results. Baste meats with barbecue sauce or honey in the last few minutes of cooking.

Oil is required to brown and crisp up lean pieces of meat or dishes with little or no fat. Brush a little oil on boneless chicken breasts and pork chops before seasoning, for example. Because of its higher smoke point, vegetable or canola oil is often selected to survive the intense heat of an air fryer.

Vegetables must be mixed in oil before air frying. Before air frying, we recommend sprinkling them with salt, but use a bit less than usual: The taste is exploding from the crisp, air-fried bits. Broccoli florets, Brussels sprouts, and little potato halves are all air-fried favorites of ours. When they are done, they are very crispy! Unfortunately, green beans and peppers do not get sweeter with time, although butternut squash, sweet potatoes, and beets do.

An air fryer is a small countertop convection oven that mimics deep frying without the need for oil. Instead, a fan circulates hot air at high speeds, resulting in a crisp coating produced by browning processes like the Maillard reaction.

This quick circulation crisps the food in the same way that deep-frying does, but without the oil. Some product reviewers argue that ordinary convection ovens or convection toaster ovens give superior results or that air frying is simply convection baking disguised as a fashionable new term.

Air fryers are compact, pod-shaped appliances that are designed to sit on a countertop. An air fryer has a front door that, when opened, shows a basket and a tray. The air-fried meal is placed in the basket. The tray collects debris, drips, crumbs, and so on. The open-weave basket lets hot air circulate more efficiently around the food components, which should be evenly distributed.

On average, an air fryer can cook meals for 2 to 4 serves. If you are cooking for a family, this typically means air frying in batches. While French fries, chicken nuggets, wings, and other frozen pre-cooked battered cuisine are the most popular items in air fryers, most of these devices come with instructions on how to air-fry "baked" potatoes, air-fry veggies, and about anything you can make in an oven, even cake.

An air fryer features a single fan at the top of the device. A simple air fryer's temperature regulation normally ranges from 400F to 500F.

Depending on the brand, air fryers might be unbearably loud and difficult to clean. And, as far as countertop appliances go, it is not a little one. A decent one should have a 15-inch square footprint.

An air fryer is a tiny convection oven. Its promise: to mimic the flavor and feel of your favorite deep-fried foods—without the fat and calories.

This countertop cooking equipment seems intriguing, with its promise of crispy, close-to-fried perfection. Unfortunately, some are tiny, using the same amount of counter space as toaster ovens. But how does an air fryer operate, what foods can it cook, do you need to use oil, and can it live up to the hype? Continue reading to see if an air fryer is perfect for your kitchen.

How to use your air fryer

An air fryer converts minute quantities of moisture into mist by using a heating element and a fan that circulates hot air above and around your meal. The food is placed in an air fryer basket before being placed inside the equipment. The extra-hot cooking chamber allows dry heat to penetrate the food from the outside, resulting in the classic crispy texture associated with a deep fryer bath. Cooking with an air fryer also saves time and makes cleaning simple.

It is simple to use an air fryer once you understand how it works and what it can (and cannot) accomplish. First, determine whether your air fryer has a preheat feature. Many air fryer recipes do not require preheating, but you may find that your machine's instructions require it or that you like this extra step. The good news is that preheating an air fryer takes only a few minutes, so you do not need to plan of time.

Time and temperature are the two factors that may be set on an air fryer. We enjoy the timer since, unlike an oven timer, the air fryer switches off when the timer expires, preventing your supper from burning.

Follow the directions in the recipe you are using from there. In general, you will drizzle a teaspoon or two of oil over the item you are cooking, place it in the basket, and turn it on. You will turn the food or shake the basket halfway during the cooking period. In certain circumstances, fluids and marinades fall through the basket and can be poured over the cooked food, reintroducing concentrated flavor to the meal.

How to Clean an Air Fryer

You will be cleaning your air fryer after you have used it. We have more extensive instruction for this work, but here are the fundamentals. The first step is critical: turn off the air fryer and let it cool. The pieces that pop out, such as the basket and handle, may be cleaned with soap and water. For the insides, a soft, wet cloth works nicely.

 Next, examine the heating element to check if there is any spattered food there. A toothbrush designed specifically for cleaning tiny places in kitchen equipment might be useful. If you do not clean your air fryer regularly, oil can accumulate, get sticky, and be difficult to remove (or worse, turn rancid). Remember that every model is different, so consult your owner's handbook for specific instructions – some air fryers may have dishwasher-safe detachable components, while others may not.

What Can You Make with An Air Fryer?

An air fryer is ideal for frequently preparing deep-fried foods: it can provide crispness without oil. Frozen mozzarella sticks, tater tots, frozen fries, and chicken nuggets are all good options. Air fryers are also great for preparing fried chicken, particularly amazing wings. Roasted veggies will be crispy, browned, and properly done in the middle, but you will need the same amount of oil as if your oven-roasted them. Anything that can benefit from high heat is ideal for an air fryer: cut-in-half potatoes coated in olive oil, chickpeas that become a super-crunchy snack, steaks, chops, and more. Bread and cookies may also be baked, and air fryer s'mores are a popular party trick.

Air fryer benefits

Even if you despise cooking, you have heard about air fryers. A friend has been talking about the health advantages of an air fryer, or your father has been air-fried everything recently. But have you ever wondered what makes air fryers so special? Are there any real health advantages to having an air fryer? Does using an air fryer provide the same tastes and textures as conventional cooking methods?

Howards has done the homework, and we are here to discuss the advantages of using an air fryer. We will also investigate why this culinary craze is being heralded as a new and improved cooking technique.

Air Frying ≠ Healthy

Primarily, let us dispel the myth that whatever you air-fried will be nutritious. One of the most frequently mentioned advantages of an air fryer is that it cooks healthful meals. But, unfortunately, air-fried food might still be harmful. When comparing fried meals versus air-fried foods, however, air-fried foods are frequently shown to be healthier.

If you have a doughnut, it does not matter if it is fried or air-fried; it is still a donut. Cooking with an air fryer, on the other hand, delivers the same crispiness without the use of cups of harmful oil.

Take assertions that all air-fried food is healthful with a grain of salt the next time you hear them. Remember that this is a cooking process, not a molecular change in the food being cooked.

How They Work

Let us start with an explanation of how air fryer's function. Most people have heard of an air fryer but are unaware of how it makes air-fried dishes.

We have all heard of deep-frying, which involves submerging food in a vat of hot oil, immersing it, and cooking it. An air fryer needs only a few teaspoons of frying oil since the chamber is superheated and circulates air at high speed. To achieve the desired crispiness, you substitute cups of boiling oil with circulating, superheated droplets of oil and air. This novel strategy is essential to reaping the many advantages of an air fryer.

Air Fryers can Promote Weight Loss

Diet or modifying one's diet is frequently the key to losing weight. A transition from deep-fried to air-fried items can help reduce frequent oil use and encourage healthier choices. For example, people may enjoy healthier versions of their favorite dishes without fully abandoning their health objectives because of the air fryer's ability to generate crispy foods without the need for a lot of oil. A reduced risk of heart disease is an extra advantage of avoiding deep-fried meals.

Air Fryers are Safer

One of the most underappreciated advantages of an air fryer is that it is a safer cooking method. Because an air fryer's cooking receptacle is closed and confined, you never come into touch with heat while your food cooks.

Large volumes of oil heated to extremely high temperatures are frequently used in traditional frying. However, popping oil poses a major burn risk and, if allowed to burn out of control, can result in a hazardous grease fire. Purchasing an air fryer eliminates the risk of burns and flames caused by frying oil.

They are Cleaner

The cleaning is the most difficult aspect of cooking. Even worse is having to clean up a large amount of oil. Ask anyone who has had to clear out a deep fryer how difficult it is, and you will reconsider deep frying.

Cooking using an air fryer allows you to make your food crispy while never worrying about what to deal with all that fat.

They are Fast and Convenient

Aside from requiring significantly less clean-up than traditional frying, one of the most significant advantages of an air fryer is the speed and ease with which it cooks. You set it and then forget about it.

Cooking in an air fryer evenly warms both sides. This means no turning or monitoring, allowing you to prepare other things or return to perfectly cooked food. As a result, cook times are frequently shorter than those of traditional frying or baking, allowing you more time to enjoy your meal or get on with your day.

Cons of Air Fryers

Why, with so many advantages, isn't an air fryer more widespread in homes? One explanation is that it is still a new thing in the world of cooking. People are still debating whether it is worthwhile to get an air fryer. Second, there are a few drawbacks that must be addressed. The two most common drawbacks of air fryers are that they are countertop appliances and can only cook limited amounts of food at a time.

On the other hand, Frigidaire is addressing these two major problems by being the first business to produce a kitchen range with an integrated air fryer. As a result, you will not have to add another appliance to your already congested countertop, and you will be able to air fry party-sized amounts of food. It seems like a great win all around, and it shows that air fryers are more than just a fad in the culinary world. Let us know what you think of air fryers in the comments!

Air fryer tips & tricks

Preheat the Air Fryer... Most of the time, at least

It is normal practice to preheat any cooking element. Most air fryer manufacturers recommend that the air fryer be warmed to guarantee equal frying. I do it occasionally, and my meal is still excellent when I do not. If your air fryer lacks a preheat function, set the temperature, and let it run for around 3 minutes before adding your food.

Apply oil to your items for the air fryer... Most of the time, at least

I prefer to use oil on certain dishes to help them crisp up, but not all foods require it.

You do not need the oil if your dish already has some fat on it (dark flesh chicken, ground beef, fatty pieces of meat, etc.). Oil is used on vegetables (such as my Breakfast Air Fried Potatoes) and any battered seafood (such as my Crispy Air Fryer Fish).

Grease your Air Fryer Basket

Even though your meal does not require oil, it is always a good idea to lubricate your air fryer basket.

I lubricate mine by rubbing or spraying a small amount of oil on the bottom grates. This will prevent your food from sticking.

Never use aerosol spray cans in your air fryer

Aerosol spray cans (such as Pam and similar brands) have been linked to chipping in several Air Fryer baskets.

This is because the harsh compounds in aerosol cans do not mix with the coating of most baskets. Therefore, it is essential to get a high-quality oil mister or container. I make use of the Evo Spray Bottle.

Do not overcrowd the basket

If you want your fried meals to be crispy, make sure you do not overcrowd the basket. Overfilling the basket will prevent your food from crisping and browning.

To avoid this, cook your food in batches or get a larger air fryer. My first air fryer was a Farber ware model that held four servings of wings and fries.

CHAPTER 1: Breakfast

1. Air Fryer Potato Wedges

Nutrition's Fact: Calories 211, Carbohydrates 14g, Protein 31g, Fat 3g

Preparation Time: *20 Minutes Yield: 1 Serving*

Ingredients

- 2 medium Russet potatoes, cut into wedges
- ½ teaspoon paprika
- 1 ½ tablespoon olive oil
- ½ teaspoon parsley flakes
- ½ teaspoon sea salt
- ½ teaspoon chili powder
- ⅛ teaspoon ground black pepper

Steps To Cook

➢ Preheat the air fryer carefully to 400°F (200 degrees C).
➢ In a large mixing basin, combine the potato wedges. Next, mix olive oil, paprika, parsley, chile, salt, and pepper until completely combined.
➢ Cook for 10 minutes with 8 wedges in the air fryer basket.
➢ Cook for an additional 5 minutes after flipping the wedges with tongs. Rep with the remaining 8 wedges.

2. Air Fryer Spanish Tortilla

Nutrition's Fact: Calories 209, Carbohydrates 11g, Protein 23g, Fat 4g

Preparation Time: 20 Minutes Yield: 1 Serving

Ingredients

- 1 large potato, peeled
- ⅛ cup leek, sliced into 1/4-inch pieces
- 1 tablespoon extra-virgin olive oil
- 5 eggs
- salt and ground black pepper to taste
- ¼ cup grated Pecorino Romano cheese
- ⅛ cup chopped fresh flat-leaf parsley

Steps To Cook

➢ Rinse the potato cubes and place them in a dish of cold water for about 10 minutes.
➢ Preheat an air fryer to 325°F (160 degrees C).
➢ Drain and pat dry the potatoes. Toss with olive oil in a mixing basin. Place them in an air fryer basket.
➢ 18 minutes in the oven Raise the temperature to 350°F (180 degrees C). Shake the basket vigorously. Shake the basket again after adding the leek. Cook for 3 minutes, or until the leek has softened.
➢ Meanwhile, combine the eggs, Pecorino Romano cheese, salt, and pepper in a mixing bowl, and pour into a 6-inch nonstick cake pan. Cooked potatoes and leeks should be added at the end. Place the cake pan properly in the air fryer basket. Cook for about 15 minutes, or until the tortilla has browned on top and the center no longer jiggles.
➢ Remove from the air fryer and properly set aside for 5 minutes to cool. Before serving, sprinkle with Italian parsley.

3. Air Fryer Stuffed Mushrooms

Nutrition's Fact: Calories 201, Carbohydrates 12g, Protein 25g, Fat 3g

Preparation Time: 20 Minutes Yield: 1 Serving

Ingredients

- 1 (16 ounces) package whole white button mushrooms
- 4 ounces cream cheese
- 2 scallions
- ¼ cup finely shredded sharp Cheddar cheese
- 1 pinch salt
- ¼ teaspoon ground paprika
- cooking spray

Steps To Cook

➢ Gently clean the mushrooms with a moist towel. Remove and discard the stems.
➢ Separate the white and green sections of the scallions.
➢ Preheat an air fryer to 360°F (182 degrees C).
➢ In a small mixing dish, combine cream cheese, Cheddar cheese, the white sections of the scallions, paprika, and salt. Stuff the filling into the mushrooms, pushing it in with the back of a small spoon to fill the cavity.
➢ Cooking sprays the air fryer basket and place the mushrooms inside. You may need to perform two batches depending on the size of your air fryer.
➢ Cook for 8 minutes or until the filling is gently browned. Rep with the remaining mushrooms.
➢ Allow mushrooms to cool for 5 minutes before serving, then top with scallion greens.

4. Air Fryer Roasted Almonds

Nutrition's Fact: Calories 208, Carbohydrates 9g, Protein 28g, Fat 4g

Preparation Time: *20 Minutes Yield: 1 Serving*

Ingredients

- 1 tablespoon olive oil
- ¾ tablespoon very hot water
- 2 cups raw almonds
- ¾ teaspoon Himalayan pink salt
- salt to taste

Steps To Cook

➢ Per the manufacturer's recommendations, preheat an air fryer to 325–350°F (165–175°C). Line a baking pan with aluminum foil.

➢ Mix water and 3/4 teaspoon pink salt; mix until the salt is dissolved.

➢ Pour saltwater over almonds in a medium ceramic or stainless mixing bowl, whisk until coated. Almonds should be uniformly distributed on the prepared baking sheet.

➢ Bake for 6 to 7 minutes in a preheated air fryer. Remove the baking sheet, toss the almonds, and return to the air fryer for 5 to 6 minutes longer, or until the almonds become brown on the interior.

➢ Return the almonds to the mixing bowl, add the olive oil and salt, and toss until evenly covered. Allow cooling completely before serving, either in the bowl or on the counter.

5. Air Fryer Keto Thumbprint Cookies

Nutrition's Fact: Calories 205, Carbohydrates 12g, Protein 23g, Fat 2g

Preparation Time: *20 Minutes Yield: 1 Serving*

Ingredients

- 1 cup almond flour
- 3 tablespoons low-calorie natural sweetener
- 2 ounces cream cheese, softened
- 1 egg
- 3 ½ tablespoons reduced-sugar raspberry preserves
- 1 teaspoon baking powder

Steps To Cook

➢ In a mixing bowl, combine the flour, cream cheese, sweetener, egg, and baking powder until a moist dough forms.
➢ Place the bowl in the freezer for 20 minutes or until the dough is cold enough to shape into balls.
➢ Preheat an air fryer properly to 400°F (200°C) according to the manufacturer's instructions. Then, using parchment paper, line the basket.
➢ Roll the dough into ten balls and set them in the prepared basket. In the center of each cookie, make a thumbprint. Fill each indentation with 1 spoonful of preserves.
➢ Cook for 7 minutes in a warm air fryer until the edges are golden brown.
➢ Cool the cookies entirely before removing them from the parchment paper, about 15 minutes, or they will crumble.

CHAPTER 2:
Vegetables

6. Roasted Rainbow Vegetables in the Air Fryer

Nutrition's Fact: Calories 211, Carbohydrates 14g, Protein 31g, Fat 3g

Preparation Time: 20 Minutes Yield: 1 Serving

Ingredients

- 1 yellow summer squash, cut into 1-inch pieces
- 1 red bell pepper, seeded
- 1 tablespoon extra-virgin olive oil
- 1 zucchini, cut into 1-inch pieces
- ½ sweet onion, cut into 1-inch wedges
- 4 ounces fresh mushrooms, cleaned and halved
- salt and pepper to taste

Steps To Cook

➤ Preheat an air fryer properly according to the manufacturer's instructions.
➤ Combine the red bell pepper, summer squash, zucchini, mushrooms, and onion in a large bowl. Toss in the olive oil, salt, and black pepper to taste.
➤ In the air fryer basket, arrange the veggies in a uniform layer. Cook until the veggies are roasted, approximately 20 minutes, stirring halfway through.

7. Air Fryer Root Vegetables with Vegan Aioli

Nutrition's Fact: Calories 209, Carbohydrates 11g, Protein 23g, Fat 4g

Preparation Time: *20 Minutes Yield: 1 Serving*

Ingredients

- ½ cup vegan mayonnaise
- ½ teaspoon fresh lemon juice
- 1 clove garlic, minced
- salt and ground black pepper to taste
- 1 tablespoon minced fresh rosemary
- 4 tablespoons extra virgin olive oil
- 3 cloves garlic, finely minced
- ½ teaspoon ground black pepper, or to taste
- 1 teaspoon kosher salt, or to taste
- 1-pound parsnips, peeled
- ½ pound baby carrots split lengthwise
- 1 pound baby red potatoes
- ½ teaspoon grated lemon zest
- ½ red onion

Steps To Cook

➢ In a small bowl, combine mayonnaise, garlic, lemon juice, salt, and pepper to make the garlic aioli; refrigerate until ready to serve.

➢ If your air fryer manufacturer suggests preheating, preheat it to 400 degrees F (200 degrees C).

➢ In a small bowl, combine the rosemary, garlic, olive oil, salt, and pepper; leave aside to blend the flavors. In a large mixing dish, combine the parsnips, potatoes, carrots, and onion. Stir in the olive oil-rosemary mixture until the veggies are well covered. Place a part of the veggies in the air fryer basket in a single layer, then add a rack and another layer of vegetables.

➢ Cook for 15 minutes in an air fryer.

➢ When the timer goes off, serve the vegetables, and keep warm, or continue cooking in 5-minute intervals until the vegetables are done and browning to your liking.

➢ Place the remaining veggies in the air fryer basket and cook for 15 minutes, monitoring doneness as required. If you have more veggies than can fit in a single layer, use the rack again. When all the veggies are cooked, serve with garlic aioli and lemon zest on top.

8. Air Fryer Pakoras

Nutrition's Fact: Calories 201, Carbohydrates 12g, Protein 25g, Fat 3g

Preparation Time: *20 Minutes Yield: 1 Serving*

Ingredients

- 2 cups chopped cauliflower
- 1 ¼ cups chickpea flour (besan)
- 1 cup diced yellow potatoes
- ¾ cup water
- 1 tablespoon salt
- ½ red onion, chopped
- ½ teaspoon cumin
- 1 clove garlic, minced
- 1 teaspoon coriander
- 1 teaspoon curry powder
- ½ teaspoon ground cayenne pepper
- 1 serving cooking spray

Steps To Cook

➢ In a large mixing bowl, combine cauliflower, potatoes, chickpea flour, water, red onion, salt, garlic, curry powder, coriander, cayenne pepper, and cumin. Set aside for 10 minutes to relax.

➢ Preheat the air fryer carefully to 350°F (175 degrees C).

➢ Coat the air fryer basket with cooking spray. 2 tablespoons cauliflower mixture, flattened in the basket Repeat as many times as the space in your basket permits without the pakoras touching. Next, spray the tops of each pakora with nonstick cooking spray.

➢ 8 minutes in the oven Cook for an additional 8 minutes on the other side. Transfer to a plate lined with paper towels. Rep with the remaining batter.

9. Air Fryer Pork Meatballs

Nutrition's Fact: Calories 208, Carbohydrates 9g, Protein 28g, Fat 4g

Preparation Time: 20 Minutes Yield: 1 Serving

Ingredients

- 12 ounces ground pork
- ½ cup panko breadcrumbs
- 8 ounces ground Italian sausage (mild or hot)
- 1 egg
- 1 teaspoon dried parsley
- 1 teaspoon salt
- ½ teaspoon paprika

Steps To Cook

➢ Preheat the air fryer carefully to 350°F (175 degrees C).

➢ Combine pork, sausage, breadcrumbs, egg, salt, parsley, and paprika in a large mixing bowl. Using an ice cream scoop, form 12 equal-sized meatballs. Arrange the meatballs on a baking pan.

➢ Cook for 8 minutes with half of the meatballs in the air fryer basket. Cook for another 2 minutes after shaking the basket. Transfer to a serving platter and set aside for 5 minutes to rest. Rep with the remaining meatballs.

10. Air Fryer Turkey Fajitas

Nutrition's Fact: Calories 205, Carbohydrates 12g, Protein 23g, Fat 2g

Preparation Time: *20 Minutes Yield: 1 Serving*

Ingredients

- 1 tablespoon chili powder
- ½ tablespoon paprika
- 1 tablespoon ground cumin
- ½ tablespoon dried Mexican oregano
- 1 teaspoon garlic powder
- 1 teaspoon freshly ground black pepper - ½ teaspoon onion powder
- 1-pound skinless, boneless turkey breast - 2 limes, divided
- 1 jalapeno pepper
- 1 ½ tablespoon vegetable oil, divided - 1 medium yellow bell pepper, sliced into strips
- 1 large red bell pepper, sliced into strips
- 1 large red onion, halved and sliced into strips
- ¼ cup chopped fresh cilantro

Steps To Cook

➢ Combine chili powder, cumin, paprika, oregano, pepper, garlic powder, and onion powder in a small bowl. 1 lime juice squeezed over the turkey breast Season the meat with the spice combination. 1 tablespoon of oil Set aside after tossing to coat.

➢ Cover the bell peppers and onion with the remaining oil in a bowl. To coat, toss everything together.

➢ Preheat an air fryer to 375°F (190°C) according to the manufacturer's instructions.

➢ In a preheated air fryer, cook the bell peppers and onion for 8 minutes. Cook for another 5 minutes after shaking. Add the jalapenos. 5 minutes in the oven Shake the basket and arrange the turkey strips in a single layer on top of the veggies. Cook for 7 to 8 minutes with the basket closed. Open the basket, shake it to disperse the mixture, and cook for another 5 minutes, or until the turkey strips are crispy and no longer pink in the middle and the peppers are soft.

➢ Remove the fajitas from the basket and set them in a dish or on a tray. Garnish it properly with cilantro and squeeze the remaining lime juice over the top.

CHAPTER 3:
Chicken

11. Air Fryer Chicken Katsu

Nutrition's Fact: Calories 211, Carbohydrates 14g, Protein 31g, Fat 3g

Preparation Time: 20 Minutes Yield: 1 Serving

Ingredients

- 1 large egg
- 1 cup panko breadcrumbs
- salt to taste
- ¾ pound chicken breast cutlets
- 1 tablespoon barbecue sauce (Optional)
- avocado oil cooking spray
- 1 tablespoon chopped green onions (Optional)

Steps To Cook

➢ Preheat the air fryer carefully to 400°F (200°C) according to the manufacturer's instructions.

➢ In a shallow bowl or small casserole dish, softly beat the egg and season with salt. On a dish, spread out the panko breadcrumbs.

➢ Allow extra egg mixture to drop back into the bowl as you dip each cutlet. Turn the cutlets in the panko breadcrumbs to cover both sides well, carefully pushing the cutlets into the crumbs. Place on a sheet of parchment paper. Spray each side with cooking spray and set in an air fryer basket.

➢ Air-fry for 5 minutes, then turn and air-fry for another 4 minutes. Garnish with green onions and serve with barbecue sauce.

12. Air Fryer Chicken Fajitas

Nutrition's Fact: Calories 209, Carbohydrates 11g, Protein 23g, Fat 4g

Preparation Time: *20 Minutes Yield: 1 Serving*

Ingredients

- 1 medium red bell pepper
- 1 large onion, sliced into petals
- 1 medium green bell pepper
- 2 teaspoons fajita seasoning
- 3 teaspoons olive oil, divided
- 1 pound chicken tenders, cut into strips
- salt and pepper to taste
- 8 (6 inches) flour tortillas, warmed

Steps To Cook

➢ In a large mixing basin, combine the bell pepper strips and onion petals. Drizzle with 2 tablespoons olive oil and season with salt and pepper. Stir until everything is well blended.

➢ In a separate dish, toss the chicken strips with the fajita spice. Drizzle with the remaining 1 teaspoon olive oil and stir with your fingertips until evenly incorporated.

➢ Preheat an air fryer to 350 degrees Fahrenheit (175 degrees C). Cook for 12 minutes, shaking halfway through, with the chicken in the basket. Transfer to a platter and set aside while you prepare the veggies.

➢ Cook for 14 minutes, shaking halfway through, in the air fryer basket with the vegetable mixture.

➢ Distribute the chicken and veggie mixture among the tortillas.

13. Air Fryer Chicken Taquitos

Nutrition's Fact: Calories 201, Carbohydrates 12g, Protein 25g, Fat 3g

Preparation Time: *20 Minutes Yield: 1 Serving*

Ingredients

- 1 teaspoon vegetable oil
- 1 clove garlic, minced
- 2 tablespoons diced onion
- 2 tablespoons chopped green chiles
- 2 tablespoons Mexican-style hot tomato sauce
- 1 cup shredded rotisserie chicken
- ½ cup shredded Mexican cheese blend
- 2 tablespoons Neufchatel cheese
- 6 each corn tortillas
- 1 pinch salt and ground black pepper
- 1 serving avocado oil cooking spray

Steps To Cook

➢ In a skillet, heat the oil. Cook it properly until the onion is tender and transparent, 3 to 5 minutes. Cook until the garlic is aromatic, approximately 1 minute. Stir in the green chilies and Mexican tomato sauce. Combine the chicken, Neufchatel cheese, and Mexican cheese mixture in a mixing bowl. Cook and then stir for 3 minutes, or until the cheeses have melted and the mixture is well warmed. Season with salt and pepper to taste.

➢ Heat tortillas in a pan or directly on the gas stove grates till warm and flexible. Fill each tortilla with 3 tablespoons of the chicken mixture. Roll into taquitos after folding over.

➢ Preheat an air fryer properly to 400°F (200 degrees C).

➢ Place the taquitos in the air fryer basket without touching and spritz with avocado oil. If necessary, cook in batches. Cook it for 6 to 9 minutes, or until golden brown and crispy. Turn the taquitos over, spray with avocado oil, and continue to air fry for 3 to 5 minutes.

14. Air Fryer Chicken Thighs

Nutrition's Fact: Calories 208, Carbohydrates 9g, Protein 28g, Fat 4g

Preparation Time: *20 Minutes Yield: 1 Serving*

Ingredients

- 4 skin-on, boneless chicken thighs
- 1 teaspoon smoked paprika
- 2 teaspoons extra-virgin olive oil
- ¾ teaspoon garlic powder
- ½ teaspoon ground black pepper
- ½ teaspoon salt

Steps To Cook

➢ Preheat an air fryer to 400°F (200 degrees C).

➢ Dry the chicken thighs with a paper towel and brush the skin side with olive oil. Arrange the chicken thighs in a single layer on a platter, skin side down.

➢ In a mixing dish, combine the smoked paprika, garlic powder, salt, and pepper. Sprinkle half of the seasoning mixture equally over the 4 chicken thighs. Turn the thighs over and equally sprinkle with the remaining spice mixture. Place the chicken thighs in a single layer in the air fryer basket, skin side up.

➢ Fry in a preheated air fryer for 18 minutes, or until the chicken is brown and the juices flow clear. In the middle, an instant-read thermometer should read at least 165 degrees F. (74 degrees C).

15. Air Fryer Chicken Nuggets

Nutrition's Fact: Calories 205, Carbohydrates 12g, Protein 23g, Fat 2g

Preparation Time: *20 Minutes Yield: 1 Serving*

Ingredients

- 1 cup buttermilk
- 1 cup flour
- 2 pounds chicken tenderloins, cut into nugget size
- 3 tablespoons grated Parmesan cheese
- 1 tablespoon parsley flakes
- 1 tablespoon paprika
- 2 cups panko breadcrumbs
- 1 teaspoon salt
- 2 eggs
- 1 teaspoon ground black pepper
- cooking spray

Steps To Cook

➤ In a large mixing basin, combine the buttermilk and chicken and set aside while you make the seasoned flour.

➤ Combine the flour, Parmesan cheese, paprika, parsley, salt, and pepper in a large mixing bowl. Separately, beat the eggs. On a flat dish, spread out the breadcrumbs.

➤ Each chicken nugget should be dredged in flour, then in beaten egg, and finally in breadcrumbs.

➤ Preheat the air fryer carefully to 400°F (200 degrees C). Cooking spray should be sprayed on the basket. First, fill the basket with as many nuggets as you can without overflowing it. Then, spray the tops of the nuggets lightly with cooking spray.

➤ The cooking time is 10 minutes. Cook for a further 2 minutes after flipping the chicken nuggets. Repeat with the remaining nuggets.

CHAPTER 4:
Beef

16. Air Fryer Beef Wontons

Nutrition's Fact: Calories 211, Carbohydrates 14g, Protein 31g, Fat 3g

Preparation Time: 20 Minutes Yield: 1 Serving

Ingredients

- 1-pound lean ground beef
- ½ teaspoon salt
- 2 tablespoons finely chopped green onions
- ½ (16 ounces) package 4 1/2-inch wonton wrappers
- ½ teaspoon garlic powder
- ¼ teaspoon ground ginger
- ¼ teaspoon ground black pepper
- 2 tablespoons sesame oil

Steps To Cook

➤ Combine ground beef, green onions, salt, garlic powder, pepper, and ginger; mix thoroughly.
➤ Preheat the air fryer carefully to 350°F (175 degrees C).
➤ Place numerous wonton wrappers on a dish or cutting board, not overlapping them. Fill a small basin with water and place it next to the platter.
➤ Form 1 spoonful of the beef mixture into a ball and place one on each wrapper. Dip your fingers in the bowl of water and run them along the edges of the wonton wrappers. Fold the wontons in half, forming a triangle around the meat mixture. Wet your fingers with more water and squeeze the wrapper's edges together. While you construct the remaining wontons, place folded wontons onto plates, ensuring they do not overlap.
➤ Brush the wontons lightly with sesame oil on one side. Next, place a single layer of wontons, greased side down, in the air fryer basket. Brush the tops with a little more sesame oil.
➤ After 4 minutes in the air, delicately turn the wontons with tongs. Cook for 3 to 4 minutes more on the second side, or until the wontons are crispy and the edges are golden brown. Transfer the wontons to a dish lined with paper towels to cool while cooking the remainder of the wontons in batches.

17. Air Fryer Mongolian Beef

Nutrition's Fact: Calories 209, Carbohydrates 11g, Protein 23g, Fat 4g

Preparation Time: *20 Minutes Yield: 1 Serving*

Ingredients

- Meat
- 1/4 Cup Corn Starch
- 1 Lb. Flank Steak
- Sauce
- 2 Tsp Vegetable Oil
- 1 Tbsp Minced Garlic
- 1/2 Tsp Ginger
- 1/2 Cup Soy Sauce or Gluten Free Soy Sauce
- 3/4 Cup Brown Sugar Packed
- 1/2 Cup Water
- Extras
- Green Beans
- Cooked Rice
- Green Onions

Steps To Cook

➤ Coat the steak with corn starch after thinly slicing it into long pieces.
➤ Cook for 5 minutes on each side in the Air Fryer at 390°F. (Begin with 5 minutes and increase the time as needed.) I cook this for 10 minutes on each side; however, others have complained that this is too long for them.)
➤ While the steak is cooking, warm up all the sauce ingredients in a medium skillet over medium-high heat.
➤ Whisk all the ingredients together until they come to a gentle boil.
➤ Once both the steak and the sauce are cooked, lay the steak in a bowl and soak for 5-10 minutes.
➤ When ready to serve, remove the steak with tongs and allow the excess sauce to drop off.
➤ Place the steak on top of the cooked rice and green beans, and drizzle with more sauce if desired.

18. Air Fryer Beef Roast

Nutrition's Fact: Calories 201, Carbohydrates 12g, Protein 25g, Fat 3g

Preparation Time: *20 Minutes Yield: 1 Serving*

Ingredients

- 3 Lb. Beef Chuck Roast
- 1 Package Gluten-Free
- 1 Tsp Steak Seasoning
- 4 Tbsp Unsalted Butter
- 1/2 Cup Water
- Parsley or Rosemary to Garnish

Steps To Cook

➢ Begin by preheating the air fryer for about 5 minutes at 390°F.
➢ While this is heating up, evenly season the roast with steak seasoning.
➢ Set aside the gravy and 1/2 cup of water.
➢ When the preheating time is up, gently spraying the air fryer with your preferred cooking oil spray, such as grapeseed oil.
➢ Place the roast in the air fryer and cook for 15 minutes at 390°F. The exterior will be sear sealed because of this.
➢ Prepare a sheet of foil to lay the roast on after the cooking time is complete.
➢ Remove the roast from the air fryer with care and set it on the foil. Place the roast back in the air fryer after wrapping it in foil.
➢ At this time, make sure the foil is raised around the sides of the roast to allow air to flow.
➢ Pour the brown gravy mixture evenly over the meat.
➢ Place the roast on top of the butter.
➢ Cook for 30-40 minutes at 325°F, or until the internal temperature reaches at least 145°F.
➢ Allow it to rest for 5 minutes before slicing and serving.
➢ The drippings from the roast can be used to make gravy.

19. Air Fryer Beef and Bean Taquitos

Nutrition's Fact: Calories 208, Carbohydrates 9g, Protein 28g, Fat 4g

Preparation Time: *20 Minutes Yield: 1 Serving*

Ingredients
- 1 Pound Ground Beef
- 1 Can of Refried Beans
- 1 Package Gluten-Free or Regular Taco Seasoning
- 20 White Corn Tortillas
- 1 Cup Shredded Sharp Cheddar

Steps To Cook
➤ Begin by prepping the ground beef if it has not previously been done.
➤ Brown the meat over medium-high heat and add the taco seasoning according to per package directions.
➤ When you are through with the meat, cook the corn tortillas for 30 seconds.
➤ Spray the air fryer basket with nonstick cooking spray or line it with foil and spray it as well.
➤ Fill each tortilla with ground meat, beans, and a sprinkle of cheese.
➤ Wrap them securely and set them in the air fryer, seam side down.
➤ Cooking oil spray, such as olive oil cooking spray, should be sprayed quickly.
➤ Cook for 12 minutes at 390°F.
➤ Repeat with any remaining tortillas.

20. Air Fryer Beef & Bean Chimichangas

Nutrition's Fact: Calories 205, Carbohydrates 12g, Protein 23g, Fat 2g

Preparation Time: *20 Minutes Yield: 1 Serving*

Ingredients

- 1 Pound Ground Beef
- 1/2 Cup Refried Beans
- 1 Package Taco Seasoning
- 1/2 Cup Shredded Colby Jack Cheese
- Toppings - Queso, Lettuce, Tomato, Sour Cream, Salsa
- 10 Taco Size Flour Tortillas or 5 Burrito Flour Size Tortillas

Steps To Cook

➤ Brown the ground beef and season with taco seasoning according to package directions. If you have a Ninja Foodi, you may accomplish this by selecting the sauté option.
➤ When the meat is done, stir in the refried beans.
➤ Fill each tortilla with the filling and top with shredded cheese.
➤ Fold the tortilla up to ensure that all the toppings are firmly within.
➤ Use nonstick cooking spray or olive oil spray to coat the air fryer.
➤ Place the chimichangas in the air fryer, seam side down.
➤ Apply a layer of olive oil spray on them. The avocado cooking spray may also be used for this.
➤ Cook for 8 minutes at 360°F. Check on them after 5 minutes to ensure they are well cooked.
➤ When finished, they should be gently cooked on top, and the tortilla should be securely fastened.

CHAPTER 5: Pork

21. Air Fryer Pork Chops

Nutrition's Fact: Calories 211, Carbohydrates 14g, Protein 31g, Fat 3g

Preparation Time: *20 Minutes Yield: 1 Serving*

Ingredients

- 2 tablespoons brown sugar
- 1 tablespoon reduced-sodium soy sauce
- 1 tablespoon Worcestershire sauce
- 4 (5 ounces) boneless, center-cut pork chops
- 1 teaspoon lemon juice
- ¼ teaspoon freshly ground black pepper
- 1 clove minced garlic
- 1 dash Sriracha sauce (Optional)

Steps To Cook

➢ Combine brown sugar, Worcestershire sauce, soy sauce, lemon juice, garlic, pepper, and Sriracha sauce in a small bowl.

➢ Preheat an air fryer for 2 minutes at 400 degrees F (200 degrees C).

➢ Place the pork chops on a 6-inch silicone cake pan and cover with half of the brown sugar-soy sauce. Place the silicone pan inside the air fryer basket.

➢ Cook for 9 minutes in a preheated air fryer. Cook for another 9 minutes on the opposite side. Serve the leftover sauce on top of the pork chops right away.

22. Easy Air Fryer Pork Chops

Nutrition's Fact: Calories 209, Carbohydrates 11g, Protein 23g, Fat 4g

Preparation Time: 20 Minutes Yield: 1 Serving

Ingredients

- ½ cup grated Parmesan cheese
- 1 teaspoon garlic powder
- 1 teaspoon paprika
- 4 (5 ounces) center-cut pork chops
- 1 teaspoon kosher salt
- ½ teaspoon ground black pepper
- 1 teaspoon dried parsley
- 2 tablespoons extra virgin olive oil

Steps To Cook

➢ Preheat the air fryer carefully to 380°F (190 degrees C).
➢ In a flat, shallow plate, combine the Parmesan cheese, paprika, garlic powder, salt, parsley, and pepper; stir thoroughly.
➢ Drizzle olive oil over each pork chop. Place each chop on a platter and dredge both sides in the Parmesan mixture.
➢ Place 2 chops in the air fryer basket and cook for 10 minutes, turning halfway through.
➢ Transfer to a chopping board and set aside for 5 minutes to rest. Rep with the remaining chops.

23. Air Fryer Ranch Pork Chops

Nutrition's Fact: Calories 201, Carbohydrates 12g, Protein 25g, Fat 3g

Preparation Time: *20 Minutes Yield: 1 Serving*

Ingredients
- 4 boneless, center-cut pork chops, 1-inch thick
- 2 teaspoons dry ranch salad dressing mix
- cooking spray
- aluminum foil

Steps To Cook
➢ Place the pork chops on a dish and coat both sides lightly with cooking spray. Allow both sides to remain at room temperature for 10 minutes after sprinkling with ranch seasoning mix.
➢ Preheat an air fryer properly to 390 degrees F and coat the basket with cooking spray (200 degrees C).
➢ Place the chops in the preheated air fryer, working in batches if required to avoid overcrowding.
➢ 5 minutes in the oven Cook for another 5 minutes on the other side. Allow it to rest for 5 minutes on a foil-covered dish before serving.

24. Air Fryer Dry-Rubbed Pork Tenderloin with Broccoli

Nutrition's Fact: Calories 208, Carbohydrates 9g, Protein 28g, Fat 4g

Preparation Time: *20 Minutes Yield: 1 Serving*

Ingredients

- 2 tablespoons brown sugar
- 1 teaspoon ground mustard
- 1 tablespoon smoked paprika
- 1 teaspoon salt
- ¼ teaspoon garlic powder
- ½ teaspoon ground black pepper
- ¼ teaspoon ground cayenne pepper (Optional)
- 1 (1 1/2 pound) pork tenderloin, trimmed
- 1 tablespoon olive oil
- 1 tablespoon olive oil
- 4 cups chopped broccoli florets
- salt and ground black pepper to taste

Steps To Cook

➤ In a small mixing bowl, add brown sugar, paprika, ground mustard, salt, black pepper, garlic powder, and cayenne pepper until equally blended.

➤ Brush the pork tenderloin with olive oil until it is evenly covered. Rub the spice mixture all over the tenderloin and set aside for 5 minutes.

➤ Preheat an air fryer to 400°F (200 degrees C).

➤ Place the tenderloin in the air fryer basket and cook for 20 minutes, undisturbed, in the preheated air fryer.

➤ In the meantime, arrange the broccoli in a microwave-safe bowl. Microwave on high for 3 minutes, or until tender. Season with salt and pepper after adding the olive oil.

➤ Place the tenderloin on a cutting board and set it aside for 10 minutes before slicing.

➤ Place the broccoli in the air fryer basket while the tenderloin is resting. Cook for 10 minutes, shaking the basket halfway during the cooking time.

25. Breaded Air Fryer Pork Chops

Nutrition's Fact: Calories 205, Carbohydrates 12g, Protein 23g, Fat 2g

Preparation Time: *20 Minutes Yield: 1 Serving*

Ingredients

- 4 boneless, center-cut pork chops, 1-inch thick
- 1 ½ cups cheese and garlic-flavored croutons
- 1 teaspoon Cajun seasoning
- cooking spray
- 2 eggs

Steps To Cook

➤ Preheat the air fryer carefully to 390°F (200 degrees C).
➤ Season both sides of the pork chops with Cajun spice.
➤ In a small food processor, pulse croutons until finely ground, transfer to a shallow plate. In a separate shallow bowl, lightly beat the eggs. Dip the pork chops into the eggs, allowing the excess to drop off. Place chops on a platter and coat with crouton breading. Cooking spray should be sprayed on the chops.
➤ Spray the air fryer basket with cooking spray and arrange the chops inside, ensuring sure not to overcrowd the fryer. Depending on the size of your air fryer, you may need to prepare two batches.
➤ 5 minutes in the oven If there are any dry or powdery places, flip the chops and spritz with cooking spray again. Cook for another 5 minutes. Rep with the remaining chops.

CHAPTER 6:
Lamb

26. Lamb Sliders

Nutrition's Fact: Calories 211, Carbohydrates 14g, Protein 31g, Fat 3g

Preparation Time: *20 Minutes Yield: 1 Serving*

Ingredients

- 1 tablespoon minced garlic
- ¼ teaspoon ground coriander
- ¼ teaspoon ground cumin
- ¼ teaspoon ground allspice
- ¼ teaspoon ground black pepper
- 1 pound ground lamb
- ¼ teaspoon salt, or to taste
- ¼ cup sliced red onion
- 8 small slider-sized rolls, split
- ½ cup tzatziki sauce
- 1 cup baby spinach
- ¼ cup crumbled feta cheese

Steps To Cook

➤ Preheat an outside grill over medium-high heat and brush the grate liberally with oil.
➤ In a mixing bowl, combine garlic, cumin, coriander, allspice, salt, and pepper; add lamb and stir thoroughly. Make 2-ounce patties out of the mixture.
➤ Grill patties until cooked through, 2 to 3 minutes on each side, on a hot grill. In the middle, an instant-read thermometer should read at least 160 degrees F. (70 degrees C). Place the rolls on the grill and toast for 1 to 2 minutes.
➤ Make a slider by layering spinach, tzatziki sauce, a lamb patty, red onion, and feta cheese in each bun.

27. Braised Lamb with Radishes and Mint

Nutrition's Fact: Calories 209, Carbohydrates 11g, Protein 23g, Fat 4g

Preparation Time: *20 Minutes Yield: 1 Serving*

Ingredients

- 1 tablespoon kosher salt
- 1 teaspoon paprika
- 1 teaspoon black pepper
- ¼ teaspoon cayenne pepper
- 1 tablespoon olive oil
- 4 (10 ounces) lamb shoulder chops
- ⅓ cup sherry vinegar
- 4 oil-packed anchovy fillets
- 2 tablespoons white sugar
- 5 fresh mint leaves, finely sliced
- 1 ½ cups low-sodium chicken broth
- ¼ teaspoon ground cinnamon
- 2 teaspoons minced fresh rosemary - 2 bunches of breakfast radishes, rinsed and trimmed
- 1 tablespoon cold butter

Steps To Cook

➢ Preheat the oven to 275°F (135 degrees C). Combine the salt, pepper, paprika, and cayenne pepper in a mixing bowl. Place the lamb chops on a work surface and season both sides with salt and pepper.

➢ In a large oven-proof skillet, heat the oil over high heat. Brown the lamb on both sides for 3 to 4 minutes per side. Remove the chops from the pan and decrease the heat to low. Combine the vinegar, sugar, and anchovies in a mixing bowl. Cook, often stirring to break up the anchovies. Increase the heat to medium and continue stirring until the liquid has the consistency of syrup, about 3 minutes. Mix in the chicken broth. Turn the heat up to high. Bring to a simmer with rosemary and cinnamon. Place the radishes among the cooked lamb chops in the pan. Cover. Preheat the oven to 350°F. Place the skillet in the oven. Roast for 1 1/2 hours, turning chops halfway through. Continue roasting until the flesh is barely soft and starting to separate from the bone, about 1 1/2 hours more. Turn the chops once more. Preheat the oven to 425 degrees F. (220 degrees C). Remove the skillet's lid. Roast for 15 to 20 minutes, or until the flesh is falling off the bone and fork tender. Remove the skillet from the oven.

➢ Place the lamb and radishes on a serving tray. Heat a pan over medium-high heat. Simmer the sauce until it is slightly reduced and thickened, scraping off any surface fat. Turn off the heat. Mix with the cut mint and butter. Continue to whisk until the butter melts. Serve the sauce over the lamb and radishes.

28. Bry's Chocolate Lamb Chili

Nutrition's Fact: Calories 201, Carbohydrates 12g, Protein 25g, Fat 3g

Preparation Time: 20 Minutes Yield: 1 Serving

Ingredients

- 1 medium onion, chopped
- 2 tablespoons olive oil
- 1-pound lean ground lamb
- ½ teaspoon red pepper flakes
- 1 teaspoon cumin
- ½ tablespoon dried basil
- ⅛ teaspoon cinnamon
- 3 ½ tablespoons chili powder
- 2 large cloves garlic, minced
- ½ teaspoon dried oregano
- 1 teaspoon white sugar
- 1 teaspoon unsweetened cocoa powder
- 1 bay leaf
- 1 (14.5 ounces) can diced tomatoes with juice
- salt and pepper to taste
- 4 cups red beans, with liquid

Steps To Cook

➤ Cook onions and ground lamb in olive oil in a large saucepan over medium heat.
➤ Season with red pepper flakes, basil, cumin, cinnamon, garlic, chili powder, dried oregano, cocoa powder, sugar, bay leaf, and salt and pepper to taste once the onions have softened and the meat has browned.
➤ Cook for around 1 to 2 minutes. Mix in the tomatoes and beans. Raise the heat to bring the soup to a boil. Reduce the heat to low and continue to cook for 15 minutes.

29. Lamb Ragu

Nutrition's Fact: Calories 208, Carbohydrates 9g, Protein 28g, Fat 4g

Preparation Time: 20 Minutes Yield: 1 Serving

Ingredients

- ¼ cup olive oil
- 2 pounds boneless lamb shoulder
- salt and ground black pepper
- 1 onion, cut into small dice
- 1 carrot, cut into small dice
- 1 celery rib, cut into small dice
- ½ large fennel bulb, cut into small dice
- 1 (28 ounces) can Italian-style peeled tomatoes
- 2 ½ cups dry white wine
- 4 cloves garlic, thinly sliced
- 4 sprigs of fresh marjoram
- 1 sprig of fresh rosemary
- 3 sprigs fresh thyme
- 3 cups water, divided, or more as needed - 1 orange, zested
- 3 sprigs rosemary, leaves stripped and chopped
- 1 teaspoon red pepper flakes

Steps To Cook

➢ In a Dutch oven, heat the olive oil over medium-high heat.

➢ Season the lamb shoulder with salt and pepper and fry in heated oil for 20 to 30 minutes, or until nicely browned on both sides. Transfer the shoulder to a dish.

➢ Preheat the oven to 350°F (175 degrees C).

➢ Season with salt and stir the onion, celery, carrot, fennel, and garlic into the rendered fat left in the Dutch oven. Cook and stir the vegetables in the heated oil, scraping the bottom of the saucepan to loosen any black chunks of meat that have adhered, for approximately 10 minutes or until the veggies are softened.

➢ Return the lamb shoulder to the Dutch oven, along with any liquids collected on the dish; add the tomatoes and white wine. Bundle the marjoram, thyme, and rosemary in kitchen twine and place in the Dutch oven, submerged in liquid. Cover the Dutch oven, bring the liquid to a boil, and move the pot to the oven.

➢ Bake for 1 hour in a preheated oven. Cook for 1 hour more after adding 1 cup of water to the Dutch oven.

➢ Return the lamb to the Dutch oven after transferring it to a chopping board and cutting it into tiny pieces. Stir in the remaining 1 cup of water over the lamb.

➢ Cook for another 30 minutes, or until the meat is cooked.

➢ Combine the lamb, rosemary, orange zest, and red pepper flakes in a mixing bowl. If the mixture is too thick, add additional water.

30. Lamb Souvlaki

Nutrition's Fact: Calories 205, Carbohydrates 12g, Protein 23g, Fat 2g

Preparation Time: 20 Minutes Yield: 1 Serving

Ingredients

- ⅓ cup olive oil
- 1 ½ tablespoon red wine vinegar
- 1 ½ tablespoon freshly squeezed lemon juice
- ¼ teaspoon ground black pepper
- 1 ½ tablespoon chopped fresh oregano
- ½ teaspoon salt
- 2 cloves garlic, minced
- 1 ½ pounds boneless leg of lamb

Steps To Cook

➢ Combine the olive oil, lemon juice, red wine vinegar, oregano, garlic, salt, and pepper in a medium mixing bowl. Stir in the cubed lamb until it is well covered with the marinade. Refrigerate for 3 hours or overnight.

➢ Preheat an outside grill over medium-high heat and brush the grate liberally with oil.

➢ Thread the marinated meat onto skewers, saving any marinade that remains. Grill the skewers for 10 to 12 minutes, basting with the remaining marinade and regularly flipping to ensure even grilling.

CHAPTER 7: Seafood

31. Air-Fryer Coconut Shrimp

Nutrition's Fact: Calories 211, Carbohydrates 14g, Protein 31g, Fat 3g

Preparation Time: 20 Minutes Yield: 1 Serving

Ingredients

- 1/2-pound uncooked large shrimp
- 3 tablespoons panko breadcrumbs
- 1/2 cup sweetened shredded coconut
- 2 large egg whites
- Dash pepper
- 1/8 teaspoon salt
- 1/2 teaspoon cider vinegar
- Dash Louisiana-style hot sauce
- 1/3 cup apricot preserves
- 3 tablespoons all-purpose flour
- Dash crushed red pepper flakes

Steps To Cook

➢ Preheat the air fryer carefully to 375 degrees Fahrenheit. Peel and devein the shrimp but leave the tails on.

➢ Toss coconut with breadcrumbs in a small basin. Whisk together the egg whites, salt, pepper, and spicy sauce in a separate shallow dish. In a third shallow dish, combine the flour and baking powder.

➢ Dredge shrimp in flour to gently coat; brush off excess. Dip in the egg white mixture, then in the coconut mixture, patting to help the coating stick.

➢ Place shrimp in an air-fryer basket in a single layer on a greased tray. Cook for 4 minutes, then flip the shrimp and cook for another 4 minutes, or until the coconut is gently browned and the shrimp become pink.

➢ Meanwhile, add the sauce ingredients; simmer and stir over medium-low heat until the preserves are melted. Serve the shrimp with the sauce right away.

32. Air-Fryer Wasabi Crab Cakes

Nutrition's Fact: Calories 209, Carbohydrates 11g, Protein 23g, Fat 4g

Preparation Time: *20 Minutes Yield: 1 Serving*

Ingredients

- 1 medium sweet red pepper
- 1 celery rib
- 3 green onions
- 2 large egg whites
- 1/4 teaspoon prepared wasabi
- 3 tablespoons reduced-fat mayonnaise
- 1/4 teaspoon salt
- 1-1/2 cups lump crabmeat, drained
- 1/3 cup plus 1/2 cup dry breadcrumbs
- Cooking spray
- 1/3 cup reduced-fat mayonnaise
- 1 celery rib, chopped
- 1 green onion, chopped
- 1/2 teaspoon prepared wasabi
- 1 tablespoon sweet pickle relish
- 1/4 teaspoon celery salt

Steps To Cook

➤ Preheat the air fryer carefully to 375 degrees Fahrenheit. Combine the first 7 ingredients, followed by 1/3 cup breadcrumbs. Fold in crab gently.

➤ In a small basin, combine the remaining breadcrumbs. Toss a heaping scoop of crab mixture into the crumbs. Coat gently and form into 3/4-inch-thick patties. Place patties in a single layer on a greased tray in the air-fryer basket in batches. Cooking spray should be sprayed on the crab cakes. Cook until golden brown for 8-12 minutes, rotate gently halfway through, and spritzing with more cooking spray.

➤ Meanwhile, combine the sauce ingredients in a food processor and pulse 2 or 3 times to combine until desired consistency is achieved. Serve the crab cakes right away with the dipping sauce.

33. Air-Fryer Salmon with Maple-Dijon Glaze

Nutrition's Fact: Calories 201, Carbohydrates 12g, Protein 25g, Fat 3g

Preparation Time: 20 Minutes Yield: 1 Serving

Ingredients

- 3 tablespoons butter
- 1 tablespoon Dijon mustard
- 3 tablespoons maple syrup
- 1 medium lemon (juiced)
- 1 tablespoon olive oil
- 1 garlic clove, minced
- 4 salmon fillets (4 ounces each)
- 1/4 teaspoon pepper
- 1/4 teaspoon salt

Steps To Cook

➢ Preheat the air fryer carefully to 400°F.

➢ Melt butter in a small saucepan over medium-high heat. Combine the maple syrup, mustard, lemon juice, and minced garlic in a mixing bowl. Reduce heat to low and cook for 2-3 minutes, or until the mixture thickens slightly. Remove from the heat and put aside.

➢ Drizzle olive oil over the fish and season with salt and pepper. Place the fish in the air fryer basket in a single layer. Cook for 5-7 minutes, or until the fish is lightly browned and starts to flake easily with a fork. Just before serving, drizzle with sauce.

34. Air-Fryer Fish and Chips

Nutrition's Fact: Calories 208, Carbohydrates 9g, Protein 28g, Fat 4g

Preparation Time: 20 Minutes Yield: 1 Serving

Ingredients

- 1 medium potato
- 1/8 teaspoon pepper
- 1 tablespoon olive oil
- 1/8 teaspoon salt
- 1/8 teaspoon pepper
- 3 tablespoons all-purpose flour
- 1 large egg
- 1/3 cup crushed cornflakes
- 2 tablespoons water
- 1/2-pound haddock or cod fillets
- 1-1/2 teaspoons grated Parmesan cheese
- 1/8 teaspoon salt
- Dash cayenne pepper
- Tartar sauce, optional

Steps To Cook

➢ Preheat the air fryer carefully to 400 degrees Fahrenheit. Peel and chop the potato lengthwise into 1/2-inch slices. -thick slices, cut into 1/2-in. -sticks that are thick.

➢ Toss the potato with the oil, pepper, and salt in a large mixing basin. Place potato pieces in an air-fryer basket in a single layer; cook until barely cooked, 5-10 minutes. Toss potatoes in the basket to redistribute; cook until gently browned and crisp, 5-10 minutes more.

➢ Meanwhile, combine the flour and pepper in a small basin. In a separate shallow dish, mix the egg and the water. Toss cornflakes with cheese and cayenne pepper in a third bowl. Season the fish with salt, then dip it into the flour mixture to cover both sides and brush off the excess. Dip in the egg mixture, then in the cornflake mixture, patting to help the coating stick.

➢ Remove the fries from the basket and set them aside to keep warm. Place the fish in the air fryer basket in a single layer. Cook until the fish is lightly browned and just starts to flake easily with a fork, 8-10 minutes, flipping halfway through. Do not overcook it. Return the fries to the basket to finish heating. Serve right away. Serve with tartar sauce if preferred.

35. Popcorn Shrimp Tacos with Cabbage Slaw

Nutrition's Fact: Calories 205, Carbohydrates 12g, Protein 23g, Fat 2g

Preparation Time: 20 Minutes Yield: 1 Serving

Ingredients

- 2 cups coleslaw mix
- 2 tablespoons lime juice
- 1/4 cup minced fresh cilantro
- 2 tablespoons honey
- 1 jalapeno pepper, seeded and minced, optional
- 1/4 teaspoon salt
- 2 large eggs
- 1/2 cup all-purpose flour
- 2 tablespoons 2% milk
- 1-1/2 cups panko breadcrumbs
- 1 tablespoon garlic powder
- 1 tablespoon ground cumin
- 1-pound uncooked shrimp (41-50 per pound)
- 8 corn tortillas (6 inches), warmed
- Cooking spray
- 1 medium ripe avocado, peeled and sliced

Steps To Cook

➢ Toss coleslaw mix, cilantro, lime juice, honey, salt, and, if preferred, jalapeño in a small bowl to coat. Place aside.
➢ Preheat the air fryer carefully to 375 degrees Fahrenheit. Whisk together the eggs and milk in a small dish. In a small shallow dish, combine the flour and salt. Combine panko, cumin, and garlic powder in a third shallow bowl. Shake off excess flour after coating both sides of the shrimp. Dip in the egg mixture, then in the panko mixture, patting to help the coating stick.
➢ Arrange shrimp in a single layer on a greased tray in the air-fryer basket in batches; spritz with cooking spray. Cook for 2-3 minutes, or until golden brown. Cooking spray should be sprayed on the turn. Cook for another 2-3 minutes, or until the shrimp are golden brown and pink.
➢ Serve the shrimp in tortillas topped with coleslaw and avocado.

CHAPTER 8:
Vegan

36. Air Fryer Vegan Buffalo Tofu Bites

Nutrition's Fact: Calories 211, Carbohydrates 14g, Protein 31g, Fat 3g

Preparation Time: 20 Minutes Yield: 1 Serving

Ingredients

- 1 (8 ounces) container extra-firm tofu
- 4 tablespoons unsweetened rice milk
- 4 tablespoons cornstarch
- ¾ cup panko breadcrumbs
- ⅛ teaspoon paprika
- ⅛ teaspoon garlic powder
- ⅛ teaspoon freshly ground black pepper
- ⅛ teaspoon onion powder
- ⅔ cup vegan Buffalo wing sauce

Steps To Cook

➢ Take the tofu block out of the packaging and discard the liquid. Wrap tofu in cheesecloth, set on a platter, and cover with a heavy saucepan for 10 minutes to press out any residual liquid. Remove the cheesecloth from the tofu and chop it into 20 1-inch bite-sized pieces. Place in a freezer-safe container and place in the freezer for 8 hours to overnight.

➢ Remove the frozen tofu from the freezer and defrost it on paper towels or a dry cheesecloth. Allow airing to dry.

➢ Fill a resealable plastic bag halfway with cornstarch while the tofu is thawing. Next, fill a small bowl halfway with rice milk.

➢ Preheat an air fryer to 375°F (190 degrees C).

➢ Place the tofu in the bag with the cornstarch, close, and shake to cover the tofu pieces fully. Remove the tofu and coat each piece with rice milk. In a resealable plastic bag, combine the breadcrumbs, garlic powder, paprika, onion powder, and pepper with the cornstarch residue; shake until thoroughly combined. Return each piece of tofu to the bag with the breadcrumbs, one at a time. Shake the bag until the tofu is thoroughly covered, then gently shake off the excess and lay the tofu on a wire rack while you repeat with the other tofu pieces.

➢ Cook for 10 minutes in the air fryer basket with covered tofu. To loosen the fragments, shake the basket. Cook for 3 minutes more, or until browned. Toss fried tofu bits in a basin with 1/3 cup buffalo sauce to coat. Drizzle the remaining buffalo sauce over the tofu and toss to cover. Serve right away.

37. Air Fryer Vegan Buffalo Cauliflower

Nutrition's Fact: Calories 209, Carbohydrates 11g, Protein 23g, Fat 4g

Preparation Time: 20 Minutes Yield: 1 Serving

Ingredients

- 1 ½ pound cauliflower florets
- ¾ cup all-purpose flour
- 4 tablespoons egg substitute
- 1 teaspoon garlic powder
- ½ teaspoon salt
- 1 teaspoon paprika
- nonstick cooking spray
- ¼ teaspoon ground black pepper
- ½ cup vegan Buffalo wing sauce

Steps To Cook

➤ Preheat the air fryer carefully to 400°F (200 degrees C).
➤ In a large mixing basin, combine cauliflower florets. Stir the egg replacement into the florets to coat.
➤ Combine the flour, garlic powder, paprika, salt, and pepper in a large plastic resealable bag. Shake and zip until evenly blended.
➤ 1/2 of the florets should be dipped in seasoned flour. Zip it up and shake it to coat. Fill the air fryer basket with florets. Nonstick cooking spray should be sprayed on the tops.
➤ 5 minutes in the air fryer. Cook for 5 minutes more after flipping the cauliflower over and spraying any powdery places. Repeat with the rest of the cauliflower florets.
➤ Meanwhile, prepare the buffalo wing sauce in a skillet over medium heat. Place the cauliflower in a large mixing basin. Toss the top with the wing sauce until uniformly covered. Serve right away.

38. Air Fryer Vegan Sweet Potato Fritters

Nutrition's Fact: Calories 201, Carbohydrates 12g, Protein 25g, Fat 3g

Preparation Time: *20 Minutes Yield: 1 Serving*

Ingredients

- 1 ½ cups shredded sweet potato
- ¼ cup finely diced onions
- ½ cup almond flour
- ½ tablespoon olive oil
- ½ teaspoon freshly ground black pepper
- ½ teaspoon salt
- avocado oil cooking spray
- ¼ teaspoon ground turmeric

Steps To Cook

➢ Preheat an air fryer to 350°F (175 degrees C).
➢ Combine the shredded sweet potato, almond flour, onions, olive oil, salt, pepper, and turmeric in a mixing bowl. Using a large cookie scoop, divide the mixture into 9 balls and shape it into patties. Place the patties in the air fryer basket, making sure they do not touch. Coat the tops with cooking spray.
➢ Cook in a preheated air fryer for 10 to 12 minutes, or until the cakes begin to brown on the edges. Flip the cakes over, coat with cooking spray, and continue to air fry for 6 to 8 minutes. Allow for a 1-minute rest before removing from the air fryer basket.

39. Vegan Air Fryer Taquitos

Nutrition's Fact: Calories 208, Carbohydrates 9g, Protein 28g, Fat 4g

Preparation Time: 20 Minutes Yield: 1 Serving

Ingredients

- 1 large russet potato, peeled
- 2 tablespoons diced onions
- 1 teaspoon plant-based butter
- 1 clove garlic, minced
- 2 tablespoons unsweetened, plain almond milk
- ¼ cup plant-based butter
- 6 corn tortillas
- salt and ground black pepper to taste
- avocado oil cooking spray

Steps To Cook

➤ Fill a saucepan halfway with salted water and bring to a boil. Reduce the heat to medium-low and cook until the vegetables are soft, about 20 minutes.

➤ While the potato is boiling, heat 1 teaspoon plant-based butter in a pan and sauté onions for 3 to 5 minutes, or until tender and translucent. Cook until the garlic is aromatic, approximately 1 minute. Set aside some time

➤ Drain the potato and place it in a bowl. Mash in 1/4 cup plant-based butter and almond milk, season with salt and pepper. Combine the onion and garlic in a mixing bowl.

➤ Heat tortillas in a pan or directly on the gas stove grates till warm and flexible. Place 3 teaspoons of the potato mixture down the middle of each tortilla, fold it over, and roll it up.

➤ Preheat an air fryer to 400°F (200 degrees C).

➤ Place the taquitos in the air fryer basket without touching and spritz with avocado oil. If necessary, cook in batches.

➤ 6 to 9 minutes in the air fryer until the taquitos are golden brown and crispy. Turn the taquitos over, spray with avocado oil, and continue to air fry for 3 to 5 minutes.

40. Air Fryer Venison Burgers

Nutrition's Fact: Calories 205, Carbohydrates 12g, Protein 23g, Fat 2g

Preparation Time: *20 Minutes Yield: 1 Serving*

Ingredients

- 1 pound ground venison
- 1 teaspoon seasoned salt
- 2 teaspoons Worcestershire sauce
- ½ teaspoon ground black pepper
- ½ teaspoon onion powder
- 4 hamburger buns

Steps To Cook

➢ Preheat the air fryer carefully to 400°F (200°C) according to the manufacturer's instructions.

➢ Combine the venison, Worcestershire sauce, seasoned salt, onion powder, and ground pepper in a large mixing bowl. Mix with your hands until everything is equally incorporated. Form the mixture into four patties.

➢ Cook for 6 minutes with 2 patties in the air fryer basket. Cook for 2 minutes longer after carefully flipping the burgers. Repeat with the remaining patties on a plate lined with paper towels.

➢ Serve with your favorite condiments and toppings on hamburger buns.

CHAPTER 9:
Snacks

41. Air Fryer Lemon Pepper Shrimp

Nutrition's Fact: Calories 211, Carbohydrates 14g, Protein 31g, Fat 3g

Preparation Time: *20 Minutes Yield: 1 Serving*

Ingredients

- 1 tablespoon olive oil
- 1 teaspoon lemon pepper
- 1 lemon, juiced
- ¼ teaspoon paprika
- 12 ounces uncooked medium shrimp
- ¼ teaspoon garlic powder
- 1 lemon, sliced

Steps To Cook

➢ Preheat an air fryer to 400°F (200 degrees C).
➢ Combine olive oil, lemon juice, lemon pepper, paprika, and garlic powder in a mixing bowl. Toss in the shrimp until evenly coated.
➢ Cook the shrimp in the air fryer for 6 to 8 minutes, or until pink and firm. Garnish with lemon slices.

42. Air Fryer Shrimp Fajitas

Nutrition's Fact: Calories 209, Carbohydrates 11g, Protein 23g, Fat 4g

Preparation Time: 20 Minutes Yield: 1 Serving

Ingredients

- 1 red bell pepper, sliced into thin strips
- 1 red onion, sliced into thin strips
- 1 green bell pepper, sliced into thin strips
- 1-pound uncooked medium shrimp
- 1 (1.12 ounce) package fajita seasoning mix
- 3 tablespoons olive oil
- 4 (10 inches) flour tortillas

Steps To Cook

➢ Preheat the air fryer carefully to 400°F (200 degrees C).
➢ In a large mixing basin, combine the bell peppers and onion. Set aside the shrimp in a separate dish. 2 tablespoons of fajita seasoning on top of the shrimp Season the veggies with the remaining seasoning. Drizzle 2 tablespoons olive oil over the veggies and toss to coat evenly. Stir in the remaining 1 tablespoon olive oil with the shrimp.
➢ Place the veggies in the preheated air fryer basket and cook for 12 minutes, shaking halfway through. Transfer the mixture to a large mixing basin.
➢ Cook the shrimp in the air fryer basket for 5 minutes. Cook for 3 minutes more on the other side. Distribute the veggies among the tortillas and top with the prawns.

43. Air Fryer Portobello Pizzas for Two

Nutrition's Fact: Calories 201, Carbohydrates 12g, Protein 25g, Fat 3g

Preparation Time: *20 Minutes Yield: 1 Serving*

Ingredients

- 2 tablespoons olive oil
- 1 teaspoon Italian seasoning
- 2 portobello mushroom caps, gills removed
- 6 tablespoons pizza sauce
- 2 tablespoons sliced black olives
- 5 tablespoons shredded mozzarella cheese, divided
- 8 pepperoni slices

Steps To Cook

➢ Preheat an air fryer to 350°F (175 degrees C).
➢ 1 tablespoon olive oil, rubbed on each mushroom. Fill each with 1/2 teaspoon Italian spice. Place the mushrooms, cap sides up, in the air fryer basket. 3 minutes in the air fryer
➢ Turn the mushrooms over in the basket so that the cap is facing down. Divide the pizza sauce evenly between the two mushrooms. 2 tablespoons shredded mozzarella and 1 tablespoon chopped olives on top 3 minutes in the air fryer
➢ Cover each pizza with 4 pepperoni pieces and the remaining mozzarella cheese. The pepperoni must be weighed down with cheese, or the fan will blow them off the pie.
➢ Air fried for 2 minutes, or until the cheese is melted and the pepperoni is browned.

44. Air Fryer Rosemary Garlic Baby Potatoes

Nutrition's Fact: Calories 208, Carbohydrates 9g, Protein 28g, Fat 4g

Preparation Time: 20 Minutes Yield: 1 Serving

Ingredients

- 1 ½ pounds multi-colored new potatoes, halved
- 2 cloves garlic, minced
- 2 tablespoons olive oil
- ½ teaspoon kosher salt
- 1 teaspoon finely chopped fresh rosemary
- ½ teaspoon lemon zest

Steps To Cook

➢ Preheat the air fryer carefully to 400°F (200 degrees C).
➢ In a large mixing basin, combine the potatoes, oil, garlic, rosemary, and salt. Arrange the potatoes in the air fryer basket in a single layer, not overcrowded; work in batches if required. Cook for 20 minutes, or until potatoes are golden brown and soft. Before serving, sprinkle with lemon zest.

45. Air Fryer Egg Rolls

Nutrition's Fact: Calories 205, Carbohydrates 12g, Protein 23g, Fat 2g

Preparation Time: 20 Minutes Yield: 1 Serving

Ingredients

- 2 cups frozen corn, thawed
- 1 (13.5 ounces) can eat spinach, drained
- 1 (15 ounces) can of black beans, drained and rinsed
- 1 ½ cups shredded jalapeno Jack cheese
- 1 (4 ounces) can dice green chiles
- 1 cup sharp Cheddar cheese, shredded
- 4 green onions, sliced
- 1 teaspoon ground cumin
- 1 teaspoon salt
- 1 (16 ounces) package egg roll wrappers
- 1 teaspoon chili powder
- cooking spray

Steps To Cook

➢ In a large mixing bowl, combine corn, beans, spinach, jalapeño Jack cheese, Cheddar cheese, green chiles, green onions, salt, cumin, and chili powder for the filling.

➢ An egg roll wrapper should be placed at an angle. Wet your finger and lightly wet all four sides. Fill the middle of the wrapper with about 1/4 cup of the filling. To construct a roll, fold one corner over the filling and tuck in the edges. Repeat with the remaining wrappers, misting each egg roll with cooking spray as you go.

➢ Preheat an air fryer to 390°F (199 degrees C). Place the egg rolls in the basket, making sure they do not touch; cook in batches as needed. Fry for 8 minutes, then turn and cook for another 4 minutes, or until the crispy skins.

CHAPTER 10:
Dessert

46. Vegan Jalapeno Cornbread in the Air Fryer

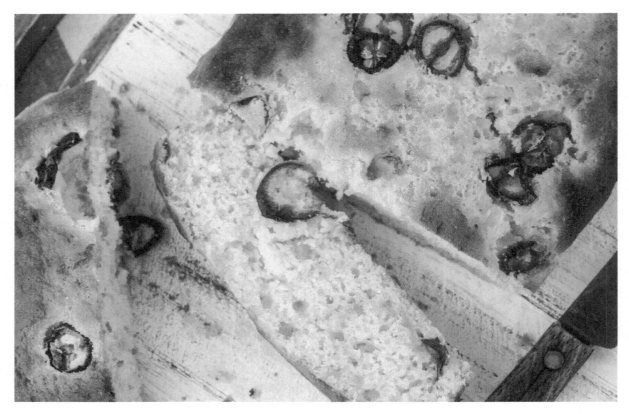

Nutrition's Fact: Calories 211, Carbohydrates 14g, Protein 31g, Fat 3g

Preparation Time: 20 Minutes Yield: 1 Serving

Ingredients

- 1 tablespoon flaxseed meal
- cooking spray
- 3 tablespoons water
- 1 cup stone-ground yellow cornmeal
- ¼ cup nutritional yeast
- ⅔ cup all-purpose flour
- 2 tablespoons white sugar
- 1 teaspoon kosher salt
- 2 ¼ teaspoons baking powder
- ½ teaspoon ground black pepper
- ⅓ cup vegetable oil
- 1 cup unsweetened almond milk
- 1 large jalapeno pepper, seeded and minced

Steps To Cook

➤ In a small dish, combine water and flaxseed meal and set aside for 10 minutes.
➤ Meanwhile, prepare an air fryer to 350°F (175°C) according to the manufacturer's recommendations. Then, coat a 6-inch heat-resistant inner pot with cooking spray.
➤ Combine cornmeal, flour, nutritional yeast, sugar, baking powder, salt, and pepper in a medium mixing bowl. Stir in the flaxseed and water combination, almond milk, and oil until it barely comes together and there are no lumps. Pour into the prepared pot and set in the air fryer; stir in the jalapeno.
➤ Cook for 15 minutes in a preheated air fryer. Remove the inner pot with tongs, turn the cornbread, and continue to air fry for another 5 minutes, or until a toothpick inserted into the middle comes out clean. Serve hot.

47. Air Fryer Salmon Patties

Nutrition's Fact: Calories 209, Carbohydrates 11g, Protein 23g, Fat 4g

Preparation Time: 20 Minutes Yield: 1 Serving

Ingredients

- ½ cup mayonnaise
- ½ teaspoon fresh lemon juice
- 1 teaspoon finely minced garlic
- 2 pinches Cajun seasoning
- 12 ounces salmon, minced
- 1 tablespoon snipped fresh chives
- 1 teaspoon finely minced garlic
- 1 teaspoon dried parsley
- ½ teaspoon salt
- 1 lemon
- 1 tablespoon all-purpose flour
- cooking spray

Steps To Cook

➢ In a small bowl, combine mayonnaise, garlic, lemon juice, and Cajun spice. Refrigerate dipping sauce until required.

➢ In a medium mixing dish, combine the salmon, chives, parsley, garlic, and salt. Mix in the flour well. Divide into four equal amounts and shape into patties.

➢ Preheat the air fryer carefully to 350°F (175 degrees C). Cut the lemon into four pieces.

➢ Place lemon slices in the bottom of the air fryer basket, then top with salmon patties. Spray the patties lightly with cooking spray.

➢ Place the basket in the hot fryer and reduce the temperature to 275 degrees F. (135 degrees C).

➢ Cook in the air fryer for 10 to 15 minutes, or until an instant-read thermometer is put into the middle of a patty registers 145 degrees F (63 degrees C). Serve with your favorite sauce.

48. Air Fryer Spicy Green Beans

Nutrition's Fact: Calories 201, Carbohydrates 12g, Protein 25g, Fat 3g

Preparation Time: *20 Minutes Yield: 1 Serving*

Ingredients

- 12 ounces fresh green beans, trimmed
- 1 teaspoon soy sauce
- 1 tablespoon sesame oil
- 1 clove garlic, minced
- 1 teaspoon rice wine vinegar
- ½ teaspoon red pepper flakes

Steps To Cook

➤ Preheat an air fryer to 400°F (200 degrees C).

➤ In a bowl, combine green beans. In a separate dish, combine sesame oil, soy sauce, rice wine vinegar, garlic, and red pepper flakes; pour over green beans. Toss to coat and set aside for 5 minutes to marinate.

➤ Half of the green beans should be placed in the air fryer basket. Cook for 12 minutes, shaking the basket halfway through. Repeat with the rest of the green beans.

49. Air Fryer Ravioli

Nutrition's Fact: Calories 208, Carbohydrates 9g, Protein 28g, Fat 4g

Preparation Time: 20 Minutes Yield: 1 Serving

Ingredients

- 1 large egg
- ¼ cup Italian-style breadcrumbs
- 1 tablespoon water
- ¼ cup freshly grated Pecorino Romano cheese
- olive oil cooking spray
- 1 (9 ounces) package refrigerated spinach and mozzarella ravioli
- 1 cup marinara sauce, heated

Steps To Cook

➢ Preheat an air fryer to 350°F (175°C) according to the manufacturer's instructions.

➢ In a small mixing dish, combine the egg and water. On a dish, combine breadcrumbs and Pecorino Romano cheese. 1 ravioli at a time, dip into the beaten egg mixture, then into the bread crumb mixture, pressing to coat. Place the ravioli on a platter and continue with the remaining ravioli. Coat the ravioli lightly with cooking spray.

➢ Place as many raviolis as you can in the air fryer basket without them overlapping.

➢ Cook for 6 minutes in a hot air fryer. Cook for 4 minutes longer after flipping the ravioli with tongs. Remove the ravioli from the air fryer and repeat with the remaining ravioli. For dipping, serve with your favorite marinara sauce.

50. Air Fryer Burgers

Nutrition's Fact: Calories 205, Carbohydrates 12g, Protein 23g, Fat 2g

Preparation Time: *20 Minutes Yield: 1 Serving*

Ingredients

- 1 (16 ounces) package ground beef
- 1 teaspoon minced garlic
- ½ red onion, diced
- 1 teaspoon salt
- 1 teaspoon Worcestershire sauce
- 1 teaspoon ground black pepper
- 1 teaspoon hot English mustard

Steps To Cook

➢ Preheat an air fryer to 350°F (175 degrees C).
➢ Combine the meat, red onion, garlic, salt, pepper, Worcestershire sauce, and English mustard in a mixing bowl.
➢ Patties may be made by flattening a ball of ground beef with your hand and rounding the sides to the appropriate size.
➢ Cook the burgers in the preheated air fryer for about 10 minutes, or until firm and no longer pink in the middle. In the middle, an instant-read thermometer should read at least 160 degrees F. (70 degrees C).

Conclusion

Diet or modifying one's diet is frequently the key to losing weight. A transition from deep-fried to air-fried items can help reduce frequent oil use and encourage healthier choices. People may enjoy healthier versions of their favorite dishes without fully abandoning their health objectives because of the air fryer's ability to generate crispy foods without the need for a lot of oil. Primarily, let us dispel the myth that whatever you air-fried will be nutritious. One of the most usually touted benefits of an air fryer is that it cooks nutritious meals. Unfortunately, air-fried food might still be harmful. When comparing fried meals versus air-fried foods, however, air-fried foods are frequently shown to be healthier. If you have a doughnut, it does not matter if it is fried or air-fried; it is still a donut. Cooking with an air fryer, on the other hand, delivers the same crispiness without the use of cups of harmful oil. Take assertions that all air-fried food is healthful with a grain of salt the next time you hear them. Remember that this is a cooking process, not a molecular change in the food being cooked.

Made in the USA
Columbia, SC
12 December 2021